Finnigan, Joan, 1925-
  This series has been discontinued

(Fiddlehead poetry books ; 292)

Poems.

ISBN 0-920110-99-1 pa.

I. Title.   II. Series.

PS8511   C811'.54   C80-094208-6
PR9199.3.F56T54

This Series Has Been Discontinued
by

Joan Finnigan

Fiddlehead Poetry Books, 1981

Author's Notes;

Most of the poems in the first untitled section of this book, in *A Set of Marriages,* in *A Circle of Love* and in *Men* have NOT been previously published in the little magazines. *Home* was commissioned by CBC-TV for its series *This Land. A Legend from the Valley* is shortly to become a children's book.

For Bob Weaver, believer

Table of Contents

"Do Ya Mind the Time?

Badour heard all the stories,
in two languages,
double vision, nuances of ghosts,
in the lobby of his father's hotel,
the "Mighty Madawasky" of Arnprior,
McLachlin's Town,
First Dan and Second Dan,
and then no more Dans.

"Do ya mind the time Big Mick Culhane
came in from Rockingham,
along the Opeongo Line
into Davidson's Corners
himself all covered with blood,
his clothes torn to smithereens,
and him saying to the people,
"Come with me, me lads. I think
I kilt a bear with me bare hands!'?"

Badour heard all the stories
in the cocked ears of childhood,
connecting to the river below its bed,
deep in the Valley soil.

"In those days it was White Lake for whisky
and the Bellamy Road for fun. You picked up
your Whisky at White Lake. But nobody needed
directions to the Bellamy Road. Just follow
your nose. Back then, I tell ye,
there was some really good dancers.
Old Tad Box from Calabogie was one of them.
I mind the night he did a lot of dancing
and laid five women besides."

How a child listens is another country;
land-locked in netherminds,
as Badour's ears got bigger
the stories grew and grew.

"Remember Jimmy Connolly and Barney Williams
and Jack Mooney? They were all old McLachlin Men.
Well, one time Jack Mooney was five or six days
up there drinking at Mount Saint Patrick
with the Maloneys and Kinnellys
and they played a turrible trick on him
and he ran clean through to Renfrew,
five or six miles down the Opeongo Line
with the devils of Paddy's Mountain
on his tail, crying, "There's a haunt
in me bottle! There's a haunt in me bottle!
And when he got home, he didn't take a drink
for a week, he didn't either."

> In the Grandfather Almighty
> bare-fisted broadaxe days
> when men named the lakes
> and the mountains.
> Badour heard the stories.

"Do ya mind the time that Michael Godda
came home from the bush in a box?
He was foreman for Booth on the Bonnechere
and he ordered his men into a log jam
and they refused to go and he said,
"All right, you sons-of-bitches,
I'll do it myself." And he did.
And they brought him home to Dacre
in a box. The Godda women, good-lookers they were,
couldn't run the hotel without a man
and they sold to Ryans, and the Ryans
died off and went away, and it sat empty
for a long time, the biggest log lumberman's
hotel in the whole valley, and then they came
and moved it to Deep River. Shame. Should have stayed
where it belonged, where it grew up, I say-----"

> In the times in the valley
> when the hills were mountains,
> and the men were giants
> and the horses Pegasus,
> Badour heard the stories.

10

"Do ya mind the time when Paddy Cosgrove,
the Bard of Allummette went up to the Island
to see this fella named O'Kelly. It was just
about noon-time, dinnertime, you see. And O'Kelly
talked to Paddy and talked and talked
and then more or less said good-bye to him.
And Paddy went home and wrote his poem,
          'Many's a man with a hungry belly
          Has passed through the gates
          Of the Great O'Kelly'.

                    Listening to the old McLachlin men
                    in the lobby of his father's hotel
                    spitting, chewing, recounting,
                    tallying the phantom teams
                    and timbers, Badour absorbed
                    the tribal tales.

"I remember Cooey Costello of Brudenell.
He was a great old lad. Lived to be pretty near
one hundred and six, he did. And a terrible man
for the women, he was, even at the end. Why,
in his last few years they had to put a weight
on his foot to keep him at home, so they did."

                    From the times when Martin Garvie stood
                    and named the mountains —
                    Ben Bulben, the Garde Pied,
                    the Natch of the Robitaille—
                    Badour recorded the tribal glories
                    from the network of Valley clans.

"Back in them days some of the rivermen
suffered from Calumet Fever —
fear of running the slides at Calumet Island.
And one year, as I remember it well,
word come to Bill Cherry of Killaloe
that his wife was very ill, come home
at once. "Well, Cherry, who did you get
to send you that word?" the other rivermen chanted.
Cherry saw the lay of the land. And cool

11

as a cucumber, he hopped the next raft down,
rode the terrible rapids through,
got off at the bottom and waved his hat
to the doubters at the top."

French-Irish Badour,
tribal recorder,
kept the Valley Book of Kells
illuminated with mists from Newfoundout
spirits from the caves at Clontarf,
haunts from Ryan's Mountain

and one hundred proof
from the Madawasky Hotel

in his time,
Badour heard the stories
running true and clean like trout streams,
like the Kazubazie in spring,
tales like mountain run-offs,
whiter than God.

O'Kane Kielly

My father came from Ireland
but when, my god, I couldn't tell ya,
a long time ago

My name is O'Kane Kielly   and I'm eighty-eight
I was born across the road over here   there was three
families of Kiellys in the Kielly Settlement
lived right close together   just about as far
as from here to the road apart   and the other
two families started going away   and then I'd be
left alone, myself and the wife and the two boys

so thirty years ago a Foley fellow lived here
and I bought this place from him and got out
to the Highway

The Kielly Settlement is right across the road over here,
three Kiellys,   there was Tom and the next was First Mick
they lived right close together   and down further
there was an aunt of mine   she was married to a Morriarity
and there was Second Mick Kielly away further down---
and Yellow Jack Kielly and Curly Jack Kielly

Never went to the shanty for anybody in my life
My father died when I was about eleven years old
It was get down to work   or get hungry
I had to work   so I've worked for seventy-seven years
I've had a good time   I enjoyed working

I used to get up here at five in the morning
and get the cows and we'd have all the milking done by eight
and get to work then   and quit about half past five again
that time it was four meals a day   my mother
used to call me to the meals with a horn
that time the horses got so used to my mother's horn
we'd be ploughing or harrowing and they'd stop
right there   the horses knew it was time for tea
breakfast about half past six   and ten or half-past ten
the horn'd blow for a snack again   half past two for tea
and then you could work as long as you'd like in the evening
but always porridge at night

Three and a half miles to school in Shamrock
kept you out of stealing and breaking
I went to Third Book   but there was no one at home
but my mother to do anything   and I had to get home
and get to work   I ploughed when I could hardly look
over the plough-handle   about eleven years old
when I'd strike a stone it would knock me down
take me a while to get up and go at it again
didn't hurt me a bit

My wife was a Hunt from the Mountain   a sister
of Father Tom   the Great Talker   they were neighbours
of ours   she lived about three miles from here
right up on this other road going to Calabogie

All the Hunts from the Mountain weren't small
My wife was a really big Hunt and J. P. Hunt
the blacksmith in Dacre   he was a big chunk
of a man, I remember

We courted for three or four years and then
we got married   she come down from the Mountain
and helped me with everything   it was really good, yes

We got married in the Catholic Church at Mount St. Patrick
I was married in a tailor-made suit   it cost me
twenty-eight dollars in Renfrew   Wilfrid Enright
stood up for us   he's dead now   and her sister
Old Enright   I miss him   he only lived
about half a mile from here and he's gone
all his big log buildings falling down

Oh, God! I was about forty when I got married
My mother, I knew my mother was dipping into everything
and I didn't want to bring anyone in to vex her
so at last I got married and they got along good,
my mother and her, and my mother stayed at home
and died at home

You've been to Mount Saint Patrick?
Well, if you haven't you've missed the best part
of your life

Mostly Catholics around here   the Bruces back here
they were Protestant   damn fine fellows
they're all out of there now   right back here
they used to be   damn fine fellows   all gone

I heard a story about Pat and Mike Daley from Ireland
they were awful lads to drink   and Irish fellows
don't drink at all   but they were two Irishmen that did
and one Saturday night, by god, they got drunk

and Holy God on Saturday night they slept
out in the ditch all night   and the next morning
they wakened up about four o'clock   and they seen
a bunch passing   and Pat said to Mike
"Where are they going to?"   and Mike said
"They're going to church, of course".
"Well," Pat said, "It's a shame for us to lie
out here all day. We should pick up and go to church".
And the two of them picked up and they walked and walked
and they weren't very sober still   · and they come
to a big square building   and they said
"Here is the church. We'll go in".   and in they went
and wasn't it a hospital   and the nurse was coming
down the hall with a bedpan   and didn't Pat put his hand
into the bedpan and blessed himself with it
And then Pat said to Mike, "Michael, me boy,
we're in the wrong church. This is a Presbyterian Church."

Farmed all my life   used to keep about ten milk cows here
when my wife was living   and sell the cream
and keep some cattle   and sell the cattle
Oh, it got pretty rough at the time of the hard times,
you know,   worked on the road   they were building
a road out there   worked on the road
for eighty-eight cents a day   look what they get now
they get about fifteen or twenty-five dollars a day
you can't get a man up here now for less
than twenty-five dollars a day for about eight hours

But eighty-eight cents and Pat Lynch done the same,
take your own lunch   ten hours   no coffee break
ten hours   seven to six   the foreman right over your back
and if you quit there was five looking for your job
and when we did work for eighty-eight cents a day
we had to wait about four weeks before we got it
before the cheque came in

But in the stores at that time you could buy stuff
and they'd charge it   but not now
they don't charge it   Sheedy's store was up here
and John Carter's at Mount Saint Patrick

Joe Blake worked in there   he came from Ireland
Mr. Carter died and Joe Blake went away
I don't know where he went   smart old fellow
nice old fellow   John Carter came from Ireland too

There's a mountain up there   Mount Saint Patrick
they called it   there was one mountain called
Kinnelly Mountain and the other one was Maloney Mountain
Mike Maloney was the last on the mountain way up here
and Dan Scully was the last on the other mountain

Dandy good farms up there,
all gone,
by god,
yes

Oh, every place it's the same
right back here about a mile there was people living
right up here there was people lived there
and when you pass this house away down here on the road
there was Kielly's lived there   Curly Jack Kielly
they used to call him

And Lynches used to live across here on the other road
about a mile from here across country and the Mulvihills
away over here   the Englishes   the Pascos
the Kinopecs (Polish)   all gone

And all the Maloneys is gone
My wife, Violet, is about ten years dead
Oh, she was fine here 'til then
I used to do the road here all the time
I used to get in some men and we'd do the road
when it would get slippey   and we done the road
this day it was all ice   and my wife said
the other two fellows I had with me they had no cook
and bring them all in and have their supper
and they stayed until about eight o'clock
and then there was a neighbour man and his wife
and his daughter come down after supper
and they wanted a game of cards and we played cards
until eleven o'clock and then she got another supper

and then about two in the morning she started
rolling with pain and my son Billy was here then
he'd a car   but there was no use
we couldn't get the pain stopped and we took her
to Renfrew to the hospital and the last word
I spoke to her when they were taking her away
in a wheelchair "How does it feel now, Violet?"
and she said, "The pain has gone away some"
and the next morning I phoned and the nurse said
"She took a little liquids this morning and she seems
a lot better"   and I went to Renfrew to mass
and the next thing the priest announced she was dead

Sunday morning, yup

I had four horses one time   two teams of horses, yes
I had some dandy horses   I liked horses
but I had to get rid of the whole thing when she died
yes, everything went   I sold my cattle horses
anything I had here   and they didn't want me
to stay alone   go into town   go into town
and I went into town to Renfrew and I stayed
five months and I said to msyelf, "Might as well
stay at home looking out on the road as stay in Renfrew
looking out at the street"   the fifth of April
I packed my bag and landed home eight years ago
and I've been here ever since

I never was sick in my life until I got this bad leg
about four years ago   the first year that I flitted
over here I had a big bunch of cattle and on this place
there wasn't stable enough and its pretty near a mile
over to where we used to live   but I left
about sixteen head of cattle over there
and morning and night I'd walk over there for five years
and often jog down a piece from where they were eating
to break water-holes for them   sometimes when the road
was too bad, I'd take the horses   my god, some mornings
we were walking the fences over

My father died of arthritis when he was forty-
he was all used up at forty-
the heart's good, the blood's good
every bit of me is good but the leg
Dr. Levine wants to operate on me
but I won't let him   there's a doctor
way down in them islands   in them Phillipines
and he's curing them   there's people that went
from here on crutches is step-dancing today
but it's two thousand five hundred dollars each
and I don't have it---that's what's keeping me here

When I was young we went to dances and dances
never a drop of whisky and we'd dance until the morning
I had a horse   a chestnut horse   and when the work was done
sometimes I used to steal the horse
my mother would give me hell to be out every night
and I'd steal the horse and have it back in the morning
before my mother got up and get to work then
no bed at all   I went to six dances in one week
and I danced until there were blue stars
in front of me

You danced in the Sammon Settlement
four or five violin players and all kinds of girls
in every house   and no whisky
lots of girls and lots of music
two Lynches, two Godda lads, two Murphy lads
and the Murphy girl could play the violin
you go to Kinnellys   you go to Christie Murphys
gou go to Goddas   you go to Hawleys
you go to Sammons

and I was in there once this summer
and there is one man living in there now
on the Sammon Settlement

you go down here onto 132
and you go a small piece up the road
and you take first turn to the right
and you go straight into the Sammon Settlement

but there's no use of going in
there's no one there
no one there
no one

all my neighoours come in and visit me
see how I'm coming   pick me up with a car
and take me where I'm going   I get the groceries myself
the lad was going to take me today   but he was hunting up
some cattle and he couldn't take me   Kinnelly takes me
and we'll go down tomorrow morning   there's none here now
of the Kinnellys   except Greg   and he can tell you a pile
of stuff about the Kinnellys   all gone now but him
Greg Kinnelly lives about two miles from here
and you just go straight up the road here
and you come to a corner and the cemetery
and you take this right hand turn up past
the Holywell Cemetery   go straight ahead
don't swing into the Holywell   go straight ahead
and he's at the dead end   up on the mountain
a bachelor   the last of the Kinnellys

I don't like it

This was the first year I didn't put in a garden
I can't stoop down for to put the potatoes in

You know, up at Mount Saint Patrick there
there used to be three stores   Mary Hunt
she was an aunt of Father Tom   she kept her store
right out from Jack Hunt's blacksmith's shop
and Carter had a store and Ryan had a store
and the only thing now is a hairdresser's
but I have no hair to take up there
and if I did it would cost me five dollars

I remember Greg Kinnelly's father used to cut
my hair   and I cut his   both for nothing
I used to cut hair for about fifteen around here
for nothing   Saturday nights

Father Harrington, Father Ryan, Father Brady,
Father Sammon   all the Holy Fathers have come
and gone at Mount Saint Patrick   every Sunday
we used to hitch the horse and buggy
and go up to church at Mount Saint Patrick
and sometimes we would even go to confession
but sure there was nothing to confess

nothing to tell at all

It is the Autumn Sun

It is the autumn sun
the finch sails through;

he is late to the fly-ways

already the yellow wings
of his breed
wend south in a cloud

surely a segment
of summoning
is within
his bright breast

but still he lingers
in the corn-stooks
by the stone house

wholly reluctant
to leave;

oh, fly, little finch

the chill of death
is hidden
behind the bright sun
glistening on the crab-apples,

earthbound
from the crooked
groaning tree

Warning for My Daughters

Beware of men
who do not drink
or dance

somewhere along the line
they perverted joy
and spontaneity

Lines for Year of the Child

Every child
rises
in dewiness

The day
dusties
him

Greedy Consumer of Life I Was

Greedy consumer of life I was,
always searching
rich fare

Now, stripped bare,
I work from joy
of little things

Wisdom of Zen,
happy my daughter
sometimes sings

The Latch-Key Kids

they stand on porches
in front of locked doors
and pound and scream
"I have to pee!"

they come in two breeds;
the attention-getters
who out of their deprivations
like rambunctious billygoats
bunt any adult surrogate
who comes near them

others are only wide-eyed,
wistful, warry,
like animals who have seen the trap
and heard it clang

these are the children who are
sad when they walk alone

the mother has her PHD in physics
which she says too frequently
"would be immoral to waste"

probably to the childrens' faces
she calls them
"precious"

Le Lac Des Trois Montagnes

the thrush
pierces
the wet
dawn

morning
laps
the rocks

in English
there are twelve
mountains

Aylmer, Quebec, 1961

All through the Ottawa Valley,
like mice in the morning grass,
people I know
and haven't seen for years
and people I've seen for years
and still don't know-
all my life-part people
are going through the motions
of opening an August Day

the old-timers sit on the park benches
hurried to death
by the young girls passing,
so scantily-clad,
sighed-for summer sculptures,
bronze relief

cathedral bells intone
an early morning finish for someone;
I wonder where he falls
and if there are loving hands
to shut his eyes and fold his arms
upon the circle
of his undeciphered struggle

a produce truck swings around the corner
loaded with crates of lettuce
for the wilted city,
cool green mockery under the noses
of the children
in the Lower Town slums
who, their innocence crisped by the heat,
are making their fire-escape climbs
to encounter a wind

the sweat-shining roadmen
shuttle their machinery back and forth
in a fog of dust and din,
another new highway
for all the old wrong turnings

A woman with vaguely familiar eyes
asks a policeman to direct her
to a house
torn down twenty years ago;
upon his news, she shrinks a little
as though she had hoped
that returning might have been mending;
the Jehovah's Witness pedlar
offers her repentance
and entry into the Kingdom of Heaven
but you can tell by her stance
she has a preference for life

Relentlessly,
the golden-rod heads in the ditches
although the town lads and their girls,
swinging their bathing-suits
to and from the water
have never for a single moment
considered the summer's end

The near-term girl with the wide walk
is as much in harmony with the August Day
as the fresh sweet corn the hawker cries
as his truck moves slowly
along the village streets
bringing the aproned women from their houses

Summer is ripe and ready to fall
and only a fool would wait here
on this corner any longer
for what is never to come again,
for what is never to come.

Timing

It was the supreme
moment
of my life

I was there
and ready
for it

Song For Simon

this morning

leave no stone
unturned

Simon, seek the miracle

all yours, my love
in summertime

and say not so

we all go,
eyeless in Gaza,

heart is the finder

Grey Cat

Oh, to have a heart
leaping as high
as the neighbour's grey cat
down in the garden
chasing the leaves
and the birds!

A Poem For Jack Bechtel

(who asked me to tell him how I see this spring)

conspirators in the hidden
tree-house of the world

we laughed together
like giddy children
in the garden

we laughed together
when Clay said that he
was cow-bird conscious
in the setting
of his spring

painter, playwright, poet,
we laughed together
smelling the narcissus

and the quiet nesting
of the coniferous dark;

Jack, coddling his beer,
had come from paintings

he leaned out of the star
behind his head,

said, "Joan, tell us
how you see this spring

Clay sees the skies
of Kitchener filled
with congregations
of petty bourgeois
cow-birds

and I see this spring
as paintings unwrested
from the tight knots
of my soul

but how do the eyes
of your poet-feelings
hear the spring tapping
on the tender chambers
of your heart?"

Oh, painter of Blair!

See me!

Touch me!

Hear me!

mother of three,
in my madness
I am the initial
cry of the world

I am the first fish
grown curious
about the land

I am the prime
mutation of the fern

I am all the birds
coming into our
cold kingdom,
shattering ice
with high sweet notes

(you know, we found
the first warbler
in an apple tree
at Conestoga

and though we three
shall all soon
lay our heads
upon the shielding grass

that tree shall be eternal
with poems and visitations
of lovers

birds and sun
shall crowd that tree
forever
as a shrine)
but that is not good enough,
Bechtel of Blair?

then I am a singing gypsy
with time for every lane;
at each cross-roads
I wander in all
directions, whistling
through garlands of leaves,
new sowings of stars

I am Beethoven's
apotheosis of the dance,
the Seventh Symphony
swelling across the fields

as his coming
from the distance

I am the shut red heart
of the mountain-ash
making secret berries
in places where he
has touched me

I am the reckless
unfolding abandon
of every leaf lapping
the amniotic fluids
of water and air

I am the little girls
skipping the sunny streets
away

I am the unwritten
songs of all the lovers,
dead, living, unborn

I am a child catching
the kisses of the rain

(any my first love,
compared to this,
was a nursery rhyme)
I am still failing
you, painter of Blair
friend of his?

you want to know
how the eyes of my feelings
hear the spring tapping
on the tender chambers
of my heart

Oh, I see it with the eyes
of a painter as though
I had come from blindness

yet in my recording brain
lies every lost lamented
spring

and I feel it
in my longing
to hold it
though nothing indicates
I ever shall

and I have its full sense
of horror in the child
who died by the roadside
all his little limbs
composed for the storm
of his parents' grief

(he lies in my tormented
vision and time
is the lover
in whose grip we wholly
finally are)

and I have tasted spring
in wild leeks
and water-cress and the sweet
grass we suck
where we lie

and I have smelled it
in the damp earth
and in his man-smell

and I have heard it
singing in our silences
and in places where he
has said "look!"

oh, Jack, laughing
in the dusky garden

do you remember how you
saw spring when you were
last locked in love?

I see it like that

and nothing like that

all gathered for me
into one frail flower

and I am ageless
as sky in the April
of this enchanting
anguish

I am arms flung
wide as the country

I am Aphrodite
in a silken nightie

and spring,
this spring
is a big a bed

as I shall need
for loving him

Pine Ridge Country

The snow tigers
tear
at the pine trees
along the ridge

a gross display
of greed,
raw upon
my eyes

Observation

I had an older friend
who told me once
that, as time goes by,
you break into running
and skipping
less and less often

I didn't believe him

I still don't

Family Reunion

My family is,
always has been,
a three-ring circus
including trapezists

at this particular reunion
we have a dog fight,
a cousin fight,
a sibling fight,
a wed-locked fight

my sister is crying
inside her secret gins;
her ex-husband
re-married today

she says she's crying
because he'll decrease
the alimony

but it's really because
something like a marriage
is never finished

life isn't long enough
for that kind of resolution

when we all go to leave
my mother unexpectedly
lapses into tears

"It's a sign I'm getting old",
she says

love for my mother overwhelms me
and I hold her alarming
frailty in my arms,
feeling birds fly up from graveyards,
feeling my arms helpless to intercede
against her distancing

floating outwards
on a trapeze
that won't return

Gatineau

The great black bears
the mountains
have gone into hibernation
just above the river

from Ottawa
to Pembroke
they have pulled
the blue blanket of the sky
over themselves

and now they are all
asleep
in the snows

Case For Justice

Let us all understand now
that the lawyers do not hold with justice
nor dispense it

let us all understand now
that the lawyers went into law
in the hope of justice for the world

they would deliver it up
the moment they had that precious diploma
in their ceremonial hands

they, having suffered early childhood deprivations
in the area of justice,
would bend their lives to convey it
to all others

yet, when he sat in his office some quiet evenings
after the staff had left
and forged cheque after cheque,
careful practised signatures of his old
and weakening clients

when he absconded with funds of the absentee
and innocent,
the Law Society of Upper Canada
(having been visited discreetly
by the upper eschelons
of the Conservative Party)
voted on his thousands of dollars
of treachery and dishonesty,
fined him five thousand dollars
delivered with a reprimandal cuff
to the right ear

and the next day disbarred an ethnic lawyer
from Timmins
who had used a client's five thousand dollars
for five days!

let us all understand now
once and for all
that the lawyers do not hold with justice
nor dispense it

Remark Overheard in the Timmins Airport Waiting for a Plane

"Well,
you can depend on it-
The pilots
of the north
are *ALMOST*
qualified."

Black Angus

The Black Angus
move
across the fall fields

reminders

that we are all eating
our way
into the slaughterhouse

Lines for the Movement

In September,
1974,
Abitibi Pulp and Paper
at Iroquois Falls
hired the first women
in North America
for their mill

a few weeks ago
MacIntyre Mines
hired women, too

a victory in the north
for Women's Lib?

not on your she-man life

they just couldn't get men
for the jobs

Sing a Song of Sixpence

Sing a song of sixpence,
A pocketful of Deans,
Four and twenty blackbirds,
The Queen is coming to Queen's.

When the pie was opened,
The Deans began to dean;
Now wasn't that a dainty dish
To set before the Queen?

Stinger was in his counting-house,
Counting up his money,
Mayor Steal was in the parlour,
Laughing at something funny.

Behold the citizens of Kingston,
Fighting behind the scenes,
Over who should have their dinner
With the Queen at Queen's.

The Queen was in the garden,
Having her first sip,
When she said, *"If I'd known the bloody fools*
were going to fight like this I would have done
like great-granpa and stayed aboard my ship!"

Sing a song of sixpence,
The Queen is coming to Queen's;
There's be a Crême de Councillors,
And a pie of Deans.

Sing a song of sixpence,
A Platterful of Snobs,
Four and twenty Social Climbers
Cooking on the hobs.

Sing a song of sixpence,
The Queen is coming to dine;
Pray, who will be invited
To sip Canadian wine?

Chris's Place at Lac Ste. Marie

Every mountain
has a window

the spring is so pure
I only want
to drink water

at night
lying
amongst the timbers,
the stars drift
through
skylights

it is not
so much the mountains
which keep
the valley
warm

it is
the valley-
people

A SET OF MARRIAGES

Little Theatre Marriage

She is very big
in Little Theatre
in our town

dark, slim,
soignèe,
meticulously groomed,
essence of cold pussy

she has a very quiet husband
who sucks on his pipe
until the blood runs down
his teeth

Two With One Blow

her husband,
it was said,
had "known" every woman
in the countryside

in her deprivation,
and cowardice,
she had turned
to her only son

who, at eighteen or so,
got sick of being used
as surrogaté,

moved in with some lads
at university
his own age;

with embarrassing regularity
she used to come to visit him,
at first checking to see
if his laundry
was properly done,
and if he was getting
the right things to eat,
his daily vitamins

but then he found
she was sleeping with
his pal Joey

two with one blow!

The Very Polite Husband

Orphaned very young,
he was brought up
by a grandmother
and two maiden aunts,

one of whom was capable
of making him say
"please"
when he was choking
on a chicken bone
and asking for water

it is no accident,
of course,
that he married
a three-headed woman
who tyrannizes him

The Coin Turned Over

He married a lesbian
and legally erased the mistake
by anulment

later,
when the hurt and horror
had mended,
he married a beautiful model
and often, in the mansion
where they lived,
particularly in the dark,
they could hear the echoes
of the first marriage

but inverted

49

Miracle

and then, occasionally, there are
the miracles of complement

he is a rotund fat-assed effeminate teacher
with flitty fallderal gestures of both hands
and feet

but by the good graces of the gods
of latent homosexuality
he found in an Alberta high school
a huge Amazon of a woman
who walks like a susquatch
and is big enough to crush him
like a spider on the sidewalk

but forbears to do so

because she loves him

after twenty-five years
it is still a marriage

still they look at one another
as though they were the New Lovers
with the old secret
just discovered

recently I went to their house for dinner
and she served the "most memorable meal"
of my life

no one could even cut the meat

yet he served it as though it were Cordon Bleu
set before kings
and heads of state

complimented her about her cooking
as though he were out of his mind

when I think of them I think
of all impossibilities

and all mysteries

Paying the Bill

When she was about forty
and beginning to crumble
he paid for five thousand dollars worth
of orthodontistry in Chicago
so that she might be more attractive
for her succession of lovers

child-like, he hoped that she
might love him for it

child-like, she laughed at him
behind his back

Unveiling

Many marriages are not unveiled
privately in the bedroom
as the myth goes
but publicly
at cocktail parties

and last week the wife of one of the Deans
at Bean's
unveiled hers

she raised her glass on high
and proclaimed,
"I hate men!
But most of all, I hate him!"

nobody even bothered to look
in the direction
of her pointed finger

they had been to these same cocktail parties
time and time
again

The New Woman

the skin specialist told me
that since the nun's habits
have been up-dated
and glamorized

he has had numbers of them in
for electrolysis

including one old girl
aged seventy-eight

my gawd!

another emancipated "married" woman
planning
infidelity!

Captain of the Ship

he has never made it

and he is fifty-three

he and his wife have lived
in the House of Silence
for fifteen years,
fifteen years of tearing each other down
with lovelessness,
all self-respect, pride, dignity,
masculinity, feminity, belief in oneself,
fulfilment of potential
damaged or destroyed

for eleven years now
he has been building a boat
in the basement

"When it is finished,"
he says,

"then I will leave"

everyone knows
he will never
finish it

everyone knows
he will never
Captain his ship

A CIRCLE OF LOVE

This is my would-be lover
he pressed his case
in an academic slum
across from City Park

I loved him for forgetting
I was old enough to be his mother;
he was a stage of my regression
after a death

I stepped back from his Adonis
persuasions

I loved myself that much

Fisher of time

fisher of time,
he slips his long beak
through waters
of my emptiness,
refills

slow eye,
such curve of neck
eases me

blue balm winds
round me,
through me

heron hiatus
of quiet
reflects the golden trees
of my mind

bell-weather of belonging
I would lie down on leaves,
draw the sky
into my lungs

roll into your arms
yes-tuned
and gut-eyed
forever

This is my beloved albino friend

this immature attention-getting
good-looking man-child

how well he delineates
Canadian identity
on his rolling rollicking road
to self-destruction!

"If I could be a writer
would I be a fucking publisher!"
he yells nationally
into the TV cameras

sometimes I feel sorry for those
who live close to him

sometimes I hate those who live
close to him

the country is killing him

the country cannot survive
without him

he therefore stays in orbit

his bright star
burning out fast

This is my beloved Peter Pan friend,
a wealthy generous Scot,
given to gossip
and expediency,
the battleground between fierce loyalty
and vengefulness,
captive of materialism
and fear of death;

a ruthless empire-builder,
he was a roué of renown
throughout the city

yet, out of his longing to love,
to truly go beyond himself
and find himself,
he came to me and said,
"You are in trouble. How much money
do you need? No conditions."

for that alone
I shall always love him;

if bad times came to him
I would go to him and say,
"You are in trouble. How much love
do you need? No conditions."

This is my beloved brown-eyed mother,
daddy's girl and therefore
unwittingly corrupted,
victim and survivor
of rural Methodism

when she is gone
wer will all laugh
again at her famous lines

(of the small town
she was trapped in)
"There is no such thing
as sin in Merrickville."

(and of my father)
"They don't give A's
for the things
YOU did best at Ottawa U."

when she is gone
we will all cry
again at her more poignant lines

(of us)
"The things I did wrong
in raising my children,
I did out of pure ignorance."

(and of her congenitally-deformed
first son)
"He keeps saying to me,
'Mother, oh, mother,
when will I marry
and have some children?'"

This is my beloved friend
my hungry Hungarian friend

his wife died young
in a foreign country
of an undiagnosed attack
of resentment
and hostility

and he has been impotent
ever since

incorruptible sign
of how much
he loved her

This is my beloved friend
whom I love too much
to take as lover

we meet as equals
in joy and love
and the kind of laughter
that comes out of that kind
of joy and love

from time to time
I am sustained
by the enrichment
of standing
shoulder to shoulder
with this man

I continue to search the earth
for his doppleganger

I think he should be cloned

Clay loves me so much,
knows me in my nuances so well
that when I came back from the fire-weed summer
he knew

without my saying a single word except
"hello, Clay"

rejoice Clay did
as only Clay can rejoice
with his eyes, eyelids,
lips, language, yes
and also with some sort
of bending contorting movement
of his whole body
as though he had a secret joy spasm
even in his bowels

now that the snow has fallen
on the fire-weed
Clay slumps there
without dancing
grabbing the back of the chair
making excuses for you

and all I can think is
"you bastard! I wish
you hadn't done this
to Clay

because Clay loves me so much
he only wants me to love
and be loved!"

I think it is Clay and I who
have a story fit for the roof
of the Sistine Chapel
one they haven't written there yet

but they will

Let the days go round my love for you. I would be
your wholly anonymous woman here with the world
of the house in my hands and flow into everyone
everywhere who has ever known it, and possess
this abiding belonging under your arm forever
like a stream returning to its source.

The garden growing overnight your favorites,
the paths I wear past the clocks in your care,
the wooden spoons I turn in the bowls, the plans
I intrigue, all these have their beginnings in you
where you begin in me, and in the nurtured continuations.

What I read is threaded through with you and where
I go is a rememberance or a hope of us , and then
there are the moments that sometimes descend
upon our souls like a holiness stone dropped
into a still-pond, like Johathan saying to me,
"Mother, I have only enough time to keep running
beautifully my one love relationship with Lisa-
that is all the time any of us ever have".

I remember so well your look when I told you that.
We were sitting on the rocks by the fire
at Hambly Lake in the silver evening together.

This is my beloved friend,
a world-renowned geneticist,
asleep now in the sculpture garden
Union Cemetery at Cataraqui

champion to the end,
when he couldn't run any more
he served aces
and played Connors at the net

the last time I saw him
he put on his Simpson-Sears wig,
held out his arms
and said,
"Here I am!--
What's left of me".

elitist in everything,
including love,
Mary will be left to put away
the problems of his unfinished
research papers,
the mystery of his crumpled
Sherlock Holmes hat

Bob will have all the time he wants now
to probe the genetic patterns of athletes,
to scour Frontenac County
for his piece
of lake-front land

those of us who loved him
will not be surprised to see him

following clues
in a country of virgin pines

MEN

André

There are times when I put on my finery
and fur hat and go to fashionable places
to dine in Toronto. You would not believe it,
seeing me au naturelle at Hambly Lake,
devouring the summer with my bare hands.
But it is, nevertheless, the gospel truth
as spoken by one who, on the couch
of Dan, Dan, the Magic Man has glimpsed God
through an opening on the ceiling of the room.

I have an old friend, first beau, confidante
of Trudeau, leader of the Bay Street parade,
who asked me to lunch last week because he had,
in an outfitter's store in Ottawa seen my daughter,
and, although he had never laid eyes on her before,
knew her by instinct to be mine. Like a reincarnation,
he said, an ESP experience he couldn't explain
to the Investors' Association.

A Teutonic star in the constellation of movers
and shakers in the loser country we call
our own, I went to lunch with him out of curiosity;
writer-voyeur, licensed user, I wanted to see
between what floors his elevator was stuck,
for what eviscerated turkey he had sold his soul.

Wellington's reeks of unlimited credit cards
and a stagnated interior decorator's good taste.
The food is mediocre but the clientele practised
in making the quick sweep of the eye
to see if Who's Who is there.

I have my own elitism. So I was unflurried
and kept my host in my eye. Over the years
since we first ambled home from Grade One together
I had often heard rumours of his arrogance,
stuffiness, and was prepared to be amused.

He lit his pipe, a pretention of minor proportions
to me, and laid his life out on the linen.
He has done well. By that I mean, he continues
to ask, "Where does the True Road lie
that I may live longer with myself in pride?"

Married thirty years ago, still married
in the sense that married means. All his children
not only continue to speak to him but bring
their wives and children to visit. Already
he has moved when he discovered that corruption
was settting in, will move again if some illness
comes to warn him that his space is wrong,
if some inner voice alarms undiscovered losses
occurring on a level still disguised.

Listening, I find myself trying to discern
at whose feet we garnered such belief
in ourselves, and hearken to an old phrase,
"Children whose fathers have power
in the community, always believe
in the importance of One".

I can see how all his critics
have wanted to cut him down

A few rare men
are like trees

they keep on growing

Albert

You keep asking why I haven't called you

You keep saying, "Why didn't you phone me
when you were in town?"

And I have finally decided to tell you
it's because
your life is a dead-end
and I don't want to be contaminated

my life is too precious now
and too little of it left
to spend time
at your mahogany bar ,
talking about your last trip to Tobago

or was it Tahiti?

Your dissertations on dry cleaning
are a bloody bore

I don't care if every dumb dog in the city
lays its dog-droppings on your doorstep

And I am not interested in bulls
and bears

We can't be held together any longer
by the fact that we went
to Bean's University together

Sorry about that

my poor little rich friend

I've found a drinking-stream

Sean Quilty

Oh, I went up the Valley
to a place called Killaloe;
We have to travel far to learn
the things we always knew

Sean Quilty, he came up to me,
the mists of Ireland in his hair,
and all his father's fathers
for generations there

Sean Quilty asked me once to dance
and when he asked me more,
I knew that we would dance again,
I knew we'd danced before.

Sean Quitty, he came up- to me,
the laughter lined his Irish face;
we had that night in Killaloe,
a meeting full of grace.

Sean Quilty swung me off the floor,
and whispered in my hair,
"When you and I were younger, girl,
I wish that I'd been there"

Sean Quilty, he came up to me,
the mists of Ireland in his hair,
and all his mother's mothers
for generations there

"Can we make up for time that's lost?"
"Alas, we never can, my lad;
when you and I were younger, Sean,
we chose the ones we have"

Sean Quilty held me in his arms
and danced me out of Killaloe;
the loving that we might have had
was what we always knew

Sean Quilty came to Killaloe,
the mists of Ireland in his hair,
and all his brother's wives
for generations there

Sean Quilty danced me round the moon,
the longing filled his Irish face;
Sean Quilty, yes, we'll meet again,
a feast of time, a wider space

Sean Quilty, he came up to me,
the laughter lined his lovely face;
we had that time in Killaloe,
a meeting full of grace

Glengarry

On every possible occasion
Glengarry
wears his tam
and clan plaids

inducing the courage
of his ancestors
before Culloden
and the Clearances

his house is rugged log

and all the fireplaces roar

what fears
raise these kinds
of defenses?

the enemy
is not
on the North Toronto
moors,

Glengarry

Dooley

When the boys on the Bank Corner
get bored with sitting there
watching the girls go by
they'd get Dooley
to dance in the middle of the street
until one Saturday night
he danced into the headlights
of a car
and all that was left
was Dooley's two shoes
in the middle of the street.

Marc

You can tell by his eyes
he has burnt his bridges
behind him

nor is it the first new skin
he has grown

when the snake eats its own tail
the necessary ruthlessness
is inderstood
only by a chosen few

rather than stagnate
he has separated

but in the territory
of concern and responsibility

he thinks his estranged wife
may yet find a way
to grow
and go forward with him

in the meantime, he does
not look backward
for a single day

the wholeness of the man
tells you he has
given away everything

when your life is real
you need very little

when it is false
you want everything in sight

in a land of charlatans
he intends to make a film
with integrity

and even more ridiculous,
with a theme of love
and courage

for the second time in my life
I think I may have encountered
someone who can
show me the way

and I am a fiddle
of fright

Harry

Harry, Harry
the Cross-Reference King
moves one hundred thousand miles
about this country every year,
collecting the history of our follies
and our grandeurs

Harry, Harry,
has his own chronicles,
foolish and grand

his wife, he says consistently,
was frigidified
by a Presbyterian up-bringing
and only goes to bed with him
once a month-
if that

(and you wouldn't believe the number
of women who believe him!)

in his suffering
he is forced to find
bed partners from Vancouver to St. John's-
the old dog-eared tale
of the man married
to the mother-figure lady
who allows him exactly what he chose her for-
free-ranging and never any demands
upon the quality of love

Harry, Harry
King of the One-Night Stands
defends himself by being on the move

a salaried folk-singer
"going down the road"
perpetually

(and soon to be pathetic)

Harry, Harry,
the drought-child,
walking his Cross-Reference world
in a miniature garden

a woman would have to bend down
to love him

Joe

Do not mistake his standing straight
for an inability to lean

do not mistake his pride
for arrogance

do not mistake his gentleness
for weakness

do not mistake his achievement
for ambition

do not mistake his committment to himself
for selfishness

do not mistake his generosity
for undisciplined giving

do not mistake his need
for want

do not mistake his face
for anything
but love

and confrontation

David

I sat with a miracle of a man,
aged one hundred and eleven years

I sat like a child at his knees,
remembering how Christ broke bread
and fed the multitudes

but it was not sliced,
as David David Trumble says

a child he was at eight
who, lost in the woods,
slept amongst the bears

a man he was who once
laid hands on men in lumber-camps,
axe-wounded and bleeding
to death in the shanty

I drink at the wells
of his mystery
while he cries for his first wife
who left him seventy-nine years ago

I lose time in his spirit

his eyes which can no longer see
see past mine

once the sight dims
true sight begins

I am the blind one here
straining for his vision

we hold hands

the future is his

HOME

Listen!

In every night of the world
home is love's long-standing
relationship to wind

in the first dawning
of The-Country-That-Might-Have-Been
he, mated male,
outside
he built it

as proof of promise

inside,
she lined it

sometimes singing

and home is a place where
when they know somebody is coming
by night
they always put a light
in the window

"I came here as a bride—
black caps for breakfast
and wild roses at the window."

after the honeymoon,
love is what you DO

"Josh fought the forest,
fenced our roots

the fields sprang green

we added a wing----."

Home is the place where,
when you go back there,
you don't have to knock

"Josh, I think it's time now—."

"Gently, Jenny girl,
I sent the neighbours
for Mrs. O'Donoghue.
She's on her way now."

Home is the place where people
keep vigil
by night
But, hazards of those times,
childbirth gathered in
the young mothers,
and epidemics
the young children

three to the graveyard,
Josh and Jenny,
but eight to fortune

scattered and keening
far-off
from the "green green grass
ot home"

"Home is the place where,
when you go there,
they have to take you in".

Love, for the free and married well,
is a tiny flame
you hold in your hand

you may fan it
or blow it out

every day you get up,
you make that choice,
both of you

"But, grandmother, how could
you forgive a man for bringing you
to a place like this

hair fallen out,
fingers to the bone,
bent with bearing?"

"My child, may God forgive you
for saying a thing like that!

Where else on earth
could I ever have been
but by Joshes side?"

Home is a child's memory
of strengths
and weaknesses,
of attics where things
could be kept
from generation to generation,
of somebody laughing,
of somebody crying

"We grew very old here together,
the children flown,

here, rooted way way down
we grew up to our deaths

Josh came in from the chores
one day, sat down on the side
of the bed and said,

'Jenny, my girl, I'm finished--.'

Home is the place you stay on in
after the little deaths
and the deaths

"Where did your husband say that line ran,
Mrs. Standish?"

"Well, he always said it cut clean through
the middle of the swamp
past that white pine
he left on the lane
fifty years ago---."

"We'll have to do a survey."

"Why do that? Josh knew.
He knew it well.
He drew the line--."

Home is a place you think is forever,
find it isn't

Our way of life has
fallen into decay

and home is place you
go back to sometimes
after you've flown
and built your own,
streaming tears
and singing The Hills of Home

your kids not understanding

but getting the feeling
That kind of rootedness is falling
out of fashion

the house is deserted,
the farm is vacant,
the barn is empty,
the school is boarded up

the sky is falling down

the town is bypassed,
the street is zoned commercial,
the area is expropriated

"The council will therefore
buy up your house
at the appraised value. Yes, we understand
that your parents built that home
and that you were born there
but you can find somethere else to live--
there are new apartments
everywhere in the area---."

Home is the place where you hang
your hat

"My home town? Well, I have to think
about that for a while--I lived
in Saskatoon and then we came
to Toronto, moved to Hamilton.
We were even in North Bay for a year--
I guess you'd have to say Ottawa--
we were in Ottawa for seven years."

"I grew up in a middle-class house
on a middle-class street in a crowded section
of Toronto. But, as often as I could,
I got to my grandfather's farm
near Peterborough and went wild.
No wonder they could say in those days,
'Children should be seen and not heard!'
There were so many nooks and crannies,
fields and streams, trees and gulleys
that we didn't need to be either SEEN
or HEARD for a month. Boys' adventures!
God! To this day, I wouldn't tell my parents
some of the things we did
about growing up."

Home is the place where two people
by their examples of courage
and patterns of struggle
give you the courage to struggle
in your own time

this may happen
anywhere
although it is easier

some places

than others

"We hate this goddamn purple-martin house
with its little jerry-built dormitory cells
and keep the kids quiet all the time.
We're getting to hell out soon.
We've formed with eight other couples
a co-operative building group
and we're going to build our own houses
with our own hands---just watch us!"

Home is a place where two people
want something better
for their children

this may happen anywhere
although it is easier

some places

than others

"We've never known a rooted place.
Gerry is on construction jobs
all the time and we pick up our home
and move with him. The children's
security has to be within themselves
and their personal relationships.
It can't come from rootedness
in one place---".

Home is the place where father
finds his next job

home is on the move

home is the place where two people
lay down the steadiness
underneath the unsteadiness

"What's wrong with these new townhouses
anyway? I come from row housing
in the slums of Liverpool in England
and, believe me, Nan and I think
these look pretty good.
What is it you bloody North Americans
have against semi-detached houses?"

Home is a castle with semi-detached
turrets----

"We hate being birds
in these monotonous ugly concrete cliffs.
We're both out working our asses off
to get a down payment
so we can get the kids
to hell and gone out
of this communally polluted
cockoo's nest".

Home is a place where when you come home
from school
nobody is there

Matthew and Mark,
aged eleven and twelve,
longing for adventure
and desperate to escape
the aridity of the high-rise,
Unit 7 and Unit 16,
dug for China in an eroded dell
and died there of suffocation

"Why do people look upon us
as second-class citizens?
We love living on this mountainside.
Right now two hundred and twenty-seven of us
are fighting Hydro
so that they won't be allowed
to put up a tower
that will spoil our beautiful view.
We haven't any kids
and we both work
and we CHOOSE to live here---

Lord, for this kind of living
we will have to breed toned-down men
and wired-up women!

"We're just ecstatic!
We've bought this century farmhouse
for $22,000 and we're restoring it
OURSELVES.

Home is a place where a man,
mated male,
puts a roof over the woman he loves
and thereby protects her children
as well

Leda and the Swan

its easier some places

than

others;

a primeval fact of life

fuzzied more in some places

than

others

"Fran and I decided
winter here is so difficult
what does it matter
whether you live
in a house or an apartment?
So, for six months of the year,
and Kids and Fran and I
take everything living in the caves
can offer, easy tranportation,
schools, libraries, shows, shops,
the Y, sports, parties, clubs--
and then we blow."

Where do you blow to, Mr. Standish?

"Oh, we bought paradise at a bargain price.
For only $12,000 we have a restored
log house and a hundred acres on the banks
of the Salmon River---."

Home is a place where you stay
with some people
in trust
and truth

Home is love's long-standing
relationship
to wind

A LEGEND FROM THE VALLEY

A Legend from the Valley

Once upon a time
in the Not-so-long-ago
of a beautiful new country called Canada
there lived a giant named Joe Mufferaw.

Joe was born on a farm north of Montreal.
In the tall forests and long fields of his father's farm
there was room to grow as big as his heart desired.
By the time he was twelve, Joe was able to look
over the Laurentians and see Canada in both directions.
On a clear day, standing on tiptoe, he could see
from sea to sea.

While he was reaching into manhood
and while he was growing into a giant,
Joe was very rich.
He had a father who was glad he was a man.
He had a mother who was close to the sun.
He had six brothers for racing and wrestling.
He had six brothers for teasing and tattling.
He had six brothers for loving and hating.

At sixteen Joe started to work
in the fencing-school his father ran in Montreal.
Joe was a good fencer, good enough to be a good teacher.
But no one would take fencing lessons from him.
Who wants to take fencing lessons from someone
they cannot reach?

"Go West, young man," Joe's father and mother
said to him, hating to lose him but wanting more
that he should find his way in the world.

So Joe left home and joined the Northwest Company.
He became a fur-trader as his grandfather before him
had been. He was sent to the Rat River to trap
and trade. But noone would get into the canoe
with Joe. He was fired from the Company
for being a giant.

For the first time in his life Joe was really sad.
What was a giant to do with his life?
Joe went home to his father on the farm north

of Montreal. "Father," he said, "Where am I going
to fit in?" And his father said, "Joe, my son,
they are cutting the big pine in the Ottawa Valley.
They need men who are as big as the trees there".

So Joe went to Timber Baron Daniel McLaughlin
at Arnprior on the Ottawa River. Daniel McLaughlin
was King of the Timber Barons.He had two thousand men
working for him in the bush, seven hundred teams
of horses and six twelve-horse hitches. He owned
ten farms around Arnprior and Carleton Place
where he grew the food and grain to feed
his two thousand men and his seven hundred teams of horses.

Daniel McLaughlin made so much money in wood
that he lived in a stone castle on the Ottawa River.
He bought his furniture in France, his tobacco
in England and his clothes in New York.
The only thing he bought at home in Canada
was potatoes. In those days even the rich
ate potatoes.

Timber Baron Daniel McLaughlin took one look
at Giant Joe Mufferaw and said,
"Mon Dieu! Sacre Bleu! You are just the man
I am looking for!" And he made Joe Jufferaw
the Walking Boss at four of his toughest lumber camps,
Finnerty's, Foley's, Farquhars and Farrell's.

Joe bossed the shantymen, the teamsters and the bullwackers,
the fellers and rossers, the cutters and hewers,
the scorers and scalers and sawers,
the swampers and slashers and skidders
the peavey-men, the poll-axe-men, the pike-poll-men,
the riggers and raftsmen and rivermen,
the flunkeys and filers,
the choreboys and cookees and bull cooks.

Sometimes when a Brag Load was too heavy
for the teams of horses on a big hill,
Joe helped out by giving the sleigh a shove.
Sometimes on an icy hill on the tote-roads

when a sleigh was going to run away,
Joe would throw the Groundhog Man out of his hole,
jump in himself and hold back the rear runners
of the sleigh. Many times in this way, he saved
teams of horses from being maimed and killed.
Many times in this way, he saved men, too.

But Joe's biggest job was keeping the peace in the camps.
At Finnerty's Camp the Poles fought the Finns.
At Foley's Camp the French fought the Indians.
At Farquhar's Camp, the Irish Catholics fought
the French Catholics. At Farrell's Camp,
the Orangemen fought the Micks. In the beginning,
Joe threw a few Irishmen over Ben Bulben Mountain
and a few Scots into the white water at Ferguson's Falls.
After that, peace reigned in all the lumbercamps
where Joe was Walking Boss.

Joe Mufferaw was happy at last in the Land
of the Giant Trees and the Giant Men. Six days a week,
from four in the morning until nine at night,
Joe worked very hard in Daniel McLaughlin's lumber camps.
But, on hiss day off, he had great times in the Ottawa Valley.

He used Oiseaux Rock as a diving-board
for swimming down the Ottawa River.
Often he took his weekly bath in the curtain
of the falls at Chaudiere. One time as a special treat
he caught the steam-boat to Ottawa. But he was so big
he made problems for his friend, Ithamar Currie,
Captain of the Phoenix.

So Joe went up to Mattawa where he had some Indian friends,
giants like himself. He got them to build him a canoe
that fitted his weight and height. He christened
his large canoe, Algonquin, to honour the builders.
To this day in the Ottawa Valley people still talk about how
he used to go alongside Captain Currie's steam-boat
and say to him, "Race you, Ithamar!" And Captain Currie
would take up the challenge, get up full steam.
But Joe always beat the paddle-wheeler. Only one time
did he lose. That was when a November storm
whipped the waves ten feet high on the Ottawa
and Joe lost his paddle.

On Saturday nights Joe went to every square-dance
from Killaloe to Calabogie,
from McDougall to Mount Saint Patrick,
from Combermere to Carleton Place,
from Quyon to Quilty,
from Ashdad to Aylmer,
from Wakefield to Waltham.

The girls loved to dance with Big Joe Mufferaw.
He could swing them up to the rafters.
He could swing them until their hair went straight
and they heads went dizzy. The only trouble was
that it took two days for the curl to come back
into their hair. The only trouble was that it took two days
for their heads to clear.

Now the story goes that one night after work
at Finnerty's Camp, Joe headed for the Burnstown Inn
to have a drink with the boys. He took the short-cut
through the Mountains from Blimkie's Hill
to Brudenell, and then in the back way
past the Dacre Oasis. As he galloped along,
singing to himself, suddenly a huge boulder
came crashing down from Kinnelly's Mountain
and missed killing him by mere inches.

Joe looked up and saw the dreaded Windigo
standing on a precipice above him. One glimpse only
and the Windigo disappeared into Ryan's Mountain.
Jeo never in his life had taken more than one drink,
but that night at the Burnstown Inn he was tempted
to have two.

A few weeks later on the Quebec side of the Ottawa,
Joe was hurrying down The Old Indian Trail
towards Slabtown to visit his friend, Agapit Lesperance
who kept a lumberman's hotel on Murray Street.
The Old Indian Trail ran along the fringes
of the Gatineau Hills. Joe was galloping along,

singing to himself, when suddenly, like a bull-whip,
a half mile of snake-fence wrapped itself around him
and knocked the wind out of him.

Joe caught his breath and untangled himself
just as the Windigo came crashing down through the trees.
Joe knew from his Indian friends that even giants
ran from Windigos. So Joe got up and ran so fast
he cleared the Ottawa River in one great leap
and landed on the Ontario side at Fitzroy Harbour.
The imprint of his landing can be seen there yet
near the ferry-boat docking-place.

The next night the lads at the Burnstown Inn
asked him how he did it. And Joe replied,
"Oh! It was easy! The Windigo was behind me
and I had a twenty mile run at it
before I made the leap!"

By now Joe knew that the dreaded Windigo was out to get him.
Everyone in the Ottawa Valley knew that the dreaded Windigo
was out to get him. All through the Ottawa Valley
the tale-bearers and story-tellers related the legends
of people who had been carried off by the Windigo
and never seen again. A cookee in a Gillies lumbercamp

on the Madawaska River had been eaten by a Windigo.
An itinerant preacher from Perth and Pakenham
had followed the wail of the Windigo into the woods
back of Schutt and Quadeville and never been heard of again.
The Gagan Girls of Goshen, it was told, had gone mad
because the spirit of the Windigo had entered into them.

Timber Baron Daniel McLaughlin told Joe Mufferaw,
"From now on, you must not go anywhere alone".
But Joe said to Daniel McLaughlin,
        "Just because you pay me
        Don't mean you order me;
        I am a man who would rather
        Be dead than not be free".

One night soon afterwards Joe hiked down to Hull
to court his lady-friend, Cecile Courval.
He was returning to camp very very late
on the Quebec side of the Ottawa Valley.
Just as he started up Ghost Hill
the dreaded Windigo stepped out in front of him.

The fight between the giants was on.
All the animals came out of the forests to watch.
Joe and the Windigo fought until dawn.
By then word had spread all through the Ottawa Valley.
All the people came to watch.

The Windigo was ugly and evil.
He had been beaten by his father when he was a child.
He had been left by his mother for long periods time
when he was a child.

The two giants were an even match in size.
But Joe knew that because the Windigo was so unhappy
he would tire easily. "I will wait him out,"
Joe said to himself, planning his strategy.

The famous battle between the Good and Evil Giants
lasted for days and was heard for miles
in both French and English. For a time,
Joe used a dead pine tree as a fencing-foil.
The Windigo went roilering with rage.
The dead pine tree reminded him of the stick
his father had beaten him with when he was a child.
For a time, Joe used his fingers to gouge the eyes
of his enemy. Then the Windigo went ape with anger.
The eye-gouuging reminded him of the loneliness
which had blinded him when his mother had left him
as a smallchild for long periods of time.

For his part, Joe suffered greatly from the Windigo's teeth
which had been sharpened on the bones of trappers,
lumbermen and Indians he had eaten in the woods.

Finally, the Windigo tired and Joe delivered his famous savate.
The crunch of the Windigo's jaw could be heard

from Bryson to Breckenrige,
from Carp to Clontarf,
from Shawville to Shamrock,
from Dacre to Douglas,
and even as far inland as Otter Lake
and Eganville.

Timber Baron McLaughlin, waiting in his stone castle
at Arnprior, and Cecile Courval, waiting at home in Hull,
heard the Windigo falling and breathed a sigh of relief.

The crash of the Windigo's fall made an indentation
on Highway No. 148 just below Wyman Station.
To this day, no Quebec government has ever been able
to fill it in. And it remains an eternal pothole
on the road to Mattawa and Fort Coulonge.

From their Indian friends everyone in the Ottawa Valley
knew that dead Windigos could not be buried
because they would rise again. They had to be burned.

Joe called for help from some of the other giants
of the Ottawa Valley, Mountain Jack Thomson
of Portage du Fort, the Seven Frost Brothers of Pembroke,
the Twelve MacDonnells of Sand Point,
the Giant of Cantley, Big John Horner of Radford,
Black Pat Ryan of Pontiac Village,
John Joe Turner of Quyon. They all formed
a relay team to drag the Windigo onto a plateau
in the Gatineau foothills just back of Ladysmith.

The burning of the Windigo went on for days.
Everyone came from miles around,
Denny O'Brien from the Burnt Lands of Huntley,
Pussy Paddy Maloney from Mount Saint Patrick,
the Wild Donnellys from Calumet Island,
the Witches of Waltham and Plum Hollow,
Big Mick Culhane from the Opeongo Line,
The Haggerty Boys from Brudenell,

The Shady Lady of Luskville,
Timber Barons Booth, Gilmour and Barnett,
Gentleman Paddy Dillon, King of the Madawaska,

the Fiddler of Dooney,
Rev. R. C. Horner of the Holy Rollers—
even Smiling Ned Smalinski
of Bread, Butter and Beer Street
in Carleton Place---

For the first time in the history of the Ottawa Valley,
the Ladies'Aid of Ladysmith Catholic Church
and the Ladies' Aid of Shawville Methodist
joined together and set up Baked Bean, Pie and Cake Booths
to feed the multitudes on the hillside.
And not only did the ladies of different religions
get in a lot of practise for the Fall Fair Baking Contests
but they discovered the warmth generated
by co-operation. The burning of the Windigo
brought creeds and breeds together in a Melting Pot.
And the Ottawa Valley was melded into a separate entity,
unique and special as an island.

In the beautiful new country called Canada,
Joe Mufferaw's fame spread from sea to sea.
Not only was he a giant amongst giants
but he was celebrated as a giant-killer.

To commemorate the Burning of the Windigo
Joe took a day off from the lumber camps.
He went over to Boom Island in the Ottawa River
off-shore from Sand Point and Pontiac Village.

There he picked a basket of blueberries
and a basket of cranberries. With a basket under each arm
he got on his favourite log and rode down river
to Hull to see his lady-friend, Cecile Courval.
As he rode his log down the Ottawa
people all along the shore in both Quebec and Ontario
came out to cheer him in both French and English.

Timber Baron Daniel McLaughlin raised Joe's pay
to three hundred dollars a month. Joe saved his money
and bought himself a little house in Hull to retire to.
When he was sixty, he left the lumber camps for good.
He and Cecile got married and lived together
in the little house in Hull.

Joe Mufferaw and Cecile had six sons.
And when the six sons grew up, they looked to finding work
in the woods the way their father and grandfathers
before them had done. But the timber was all gone
from the Ottawa Valley and the giant lumbermen
had all disappeared.

"Well," said the six sons of Joe Mufferaw.
Father was 'in wood'. And he always worked
in snow and ice".

And they, too, went into wood.

They, too, went to work in snow and ice.

They became the first Montreal Canadiens
and giants in their own way.

All their children's children spread
all over the beautiful new country called Canada,
north and south and east and west.
and they became the Ottawa Silver Seven,
and the Toronto Saint Pats,
and the Renfrew Millionaires,
and the Cobalt Kings,
and the Halifax Wolverines
and the Montreal Shamrocks

And their children's children spread
north and south, east and west
and they became the Kenora Thistles
and the Ottawa Senators,
and the Victoria Cougars,
and the Montreal Wanderers,
and the Moncton Hawks,
and the Winnipeg Monarchs

And their children's children spread
north and south, east and west,
and they became the Trail Smoke-eaters,
and the Winnipeg Victorias,
and the Saint John Beavers,
and the Toronto Maple Leafs

In time they even became
the Wolves from the North-West Territories